2/2014

Maple

17-2800

WOLVES IN DANGER

BY ADELE SHEA

Gareth Stevens
Publishing

Please visit our website, www.garethstevens.com. For a free color catalog of all our high-quality books, call toll free 1-800-542-2595 or fax 1-877-542-2596.

Library of Congress Cataloging-in-Publication Data

Shea, Adele.
Wolves in danger / by Adele Shea.
   p. cm. — (Animals at risk)
Includes index.
ISBN 978-1-4339-9179-0 (pbk.)
ISBN 978-1-4339-9180-6 (6-pack)
ISBN 978-1-4339-9178-3 (library binding)
1. Wolves—Juvenile literature. 2. Endangered species—Juvenile literature. 3. Wildlife conservation—Juvenile literature. I. Title.
QL737.C22 S52 2014
599.773—dc23

First Edition

Published in 2014 by
Gareth Stevens Publishing
111 East 14th Street, Suite 349
New York, NY 10003

Copyright © 2014 Gareth Stevens Publishing

Designer: Andrea Davison-Bartolotta
Editor: Therese M. Shea

Photo credits: Cover, pp. 1, 10, 12, 13, 17, 20 iStockphoto/Thinkstock; p. 5 Dushenina/Shutterstock.com; p. 6 Jean-Edouard Rozey/Shutterstock.com; p. 7 Michael Cummings/Shutterstock.com; p. 8 A.von Dueren/Shutterstock.com; p. 9 Christina Krutz/Age Fotostock/Getty Images; p. 11 Don Johnston/All Canada Photos/Getty Images; p. 14 Iakov Filimonov/Shutterstock.com; p. 15 (map) Ildogesto/Shutterstock.com; p. 15 (background) Altrendo Nature/Getty Images; p. 16 Steve Hillebrand/USFWS; p. 18 Panoramic Images/Getty Images; p. 19 John E. Marriott/All Canada Photos/Getty Images; p. 21 Comstock/Thinkstock.

Printed in the United States of America

CPSIA compliance information: Batch #CS13GS: For further information contact Gareth Stevens, New York, New York at 1-800-542-2595.

CONTENTS

Words in the glossary appear in **bold** type the first time they are used in the text.

WILD, Not Wicked

Wolves are misunderstood animals. They're often shown in movies and books as mean creatures. They look like dogs, so people compare the two. But unlike our cuddly pets, wolves are wild. They act by **instinct**. Left alone, these animals spend most of their short life just trying to find enough food to stay alive.

People and wolves haven't had a good **relationship** in the past. Wolves have been hunted nearly to **extinction**. Some populations today have healthy numbers, but many wolves are still fighting for their lives!

WILD FACTS
Once, 2 million wolves **roamed** Earth! There are perhaps 200,000 today.

Wolves are the biggest members of the dog family of animals.

SPECIES

There are at least two **species** of wolves: red wolves and gray wolves. Five kinds of gray wolves live in North America, and perhaps as many as 12 kinds live in Europe and Asia.

It's hard to tell some kinds of wolves apart, especially since different species **mate** with one another. Scientists are testing whether the Ethiopian wolf is a **jackal** or wolf. In addition, some think the eastern timber wolf isn't just a kind of gray wolf but is a separate species.

RED WOLF

▼ Gray wolves are the most common wolves.

7

Running with the Pack

Gray wolves live in groups, or packs, of six to 10. Usually the pack is made up of at least a male, a female, and their children. They hunt together. So, the larger the pack, the more food it needs.

The pack's numbers change throughout the year. A male and his mate have pups in spring. The pups begin to hunt with the pack in fall. In winter, when there's less food, some wolves in the pack may leave to find a mate or another territory.

8

WILD FACTS

A pack of about 30 wolves was spotted in Yellowstone National Park!

One male is in charge of
each pack.

9

TOUGH LIFE

Life in the wolf pack is hard, but life outside it would be nearly impossible. Wolves need to work together to find food. A major cause of death among wolves, especially pups, is **starvation**. Perhaps as many as half of all wolf pups die each year.

When the pack does find food, the wolves eat a lot. A large gray wolf may eat about 22 pounds (10 kg) of meat at a time! It may not eat again for a week or more.

WILD FACTS
Wolves can run as fast as 38 miles (61 km) per hour for a short distance.

Wolves eat deer, **caribou**, moose, sheep, and goats. They eat smaller animals when these aren't available—and even fruit.

TERRITORIES

Wolf packs live in territories in which they find food, mates, and shelter. A territory can be quite large. A wolf may travel as far as 50 miles (80 km) in a day to find food. Wolf territories in Canada and Alaska tend to be larger than territories in the lower United States.

Wolves that leave their pack may go hundreds of miles to find a new territory. Once they do, they might have to fight other wolves there. Wolves fiercely defend their lands.

WILD FACTS
A wolf howls to call its pack to get ready to hunt. A pack may howl to tell another pack to stay away.

13

BACK FROM THE BRINK

Gray wolves once lived across North America. However, they were hunted to very low numbers. They nearly disappeared from the United States in the 1930s. Antihunting laws slowly allowed their population to grow.

Today, gray wolves are found all over Canada. In the United States, they're found mainly in Alaska, Minnesota, Wisconsin, Michigan, Idaho, Wyoming, and Montana. Mexican gray wolves can be found in Arizona and New Mexico. Populations are doing so well in some places that they've been removed from the **endangered** list there.

There may be as many as 16,000 gray wolves in North America now.

North America

GRAY WOLF TERRITORY

Red Wolves

The red wolf, which is smaller than the gray wolf, has a brownish coat with black on its back. It gets its name because the backs of its ears, head, and legs often have reddish fur. Besides having a smaller body, red wolves have smaller territories and packs, too.

Red wolves can only be found in North Carolina. At one time, they were thought to be extinct! In 1980, 20 red wolves were captured and had pups in **captivity**. Now there are about 100 in the wild.

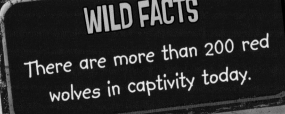

WILD FACTS

There are more than 200 red wolves in captivity today.

Scientists keep track of some red wolves in the wild with special collars and radio signals.

WOLVES VS. PEOPLE

When people enter wolf territories, the wolves are often the losers. People build on wolf land, leaving less space for wolves to hunt and find mates. Roads through wolf territories have led to many accidents and wolf deaths. And some people still hunt wolves illegally.

Many people think that wolves are dangerous animals, just waiting to attack people. This is a very uncommon occurrence. Wolves usually avoid people. They can't avoid them if they occupy the same land, though.

People should never go near wolves. They should be careful of their surroundings in places such as national and state parks.

FIGHT THE MYTH

People still trap, shoot, and poison wolves. However, some organizations are working to help farmers with livestock that wolves may attack. They're setting up alarms and fences that would keep the wolves away without harming them. They're even paying farmers for animals lost by an attack.

Sadly, the **myth** that wolves are terrible creatures lives on. You can help wolves by telling others about them—and keeping your distance!

Wolves aren't dogs. They should be respected as wild animals.

loss of land

starvation

Wolf Dangers

other wolves

hunters

farmers

GLOSSARY

captivity: the state of being caged

caribou: wild reindeer

endangered: in danger of dying out

extinction: the death of all members of a species

instinct: an inborn reaction or behavior that aids in survival

jackal: an African animal that looks like a bushy-tailed dog

mate: coming together to produce babies. Also, one of two animals that come together to make babies.

migrate: to move from one area to another for feeding or having babies

myth: a story or legend

relationship: the connection between two or more things, such as how they behave and feel toward each other

roam: to wander

species: a group of plants or animals that are all of the same kind

starvation: the state of not having enough to eat

For More Information

Books

Riggs, Kate. *Wolves*. Mankato, MN: Creative Education, 2013.

Searl, Duncan. *Wolves*. New York, NY: Bearport Publishing, 2007.

Websites

Fact Sheet: Gray Wolf
www.defenders.org/gray-wolf/basic-facts
Find out much more about gray wolves from an organization working to help them.

Red Wolf Recovery Program
www.fws.gov/redwolf/
Learn more about this endangered species.

Wild Kids
www.wolf.org/wolves/learn/justkids/kids.asp
Check out some cool wolf activities.

INDEX